This book is dedicated to my loyal and trustworthy employees, suppliers and family who helped turn my dream into reality.

Clint Pierce

The Entrepreneur's Rule Book
Copyright © 2011 by Clint Pierce.
All rights reserved.

No part of this book may be reproduced without written permission from the publisher. All recommendations are made without guarantee on the part of the author or publisher. The author and publisher disclaim any liability in connection with the use of this information.

ISBN-10: 0615524370
EAN-13: 9780615524375

Printed in the United States of America.

First Edition: October 2011

Sand House Publishing, LLC
service@sandhousepublishing.com

THE ENTREPRENEUR'S
RULE BOOK

Simple, Reliable Rules for Creating a Successful Business

BY CLINT PIERCE
WITH SUSAN SANTUCCI

Believe In Your Success!
Clint Pierce

TABLE OF CONTENTS

INTRODUCTION ix

Part One: Believe in Your Success 1

RULE #1   BELIEVE IN YOURSELF   3

RULE #2   PLAN OUT YOUR ENTIRE BUSINESS BEFORE LEAVING YOUR 9-5   7

RULE #3   ENVISION YOUR SUCCESS   13

Part Two: Have a Game Plan 17

RULE #4   WRITE A SIMPLE BUSINESS PLAN   19

RULE #5   THE NO DEBT ENTREPRENEUR   23

RULE #6   PUT YOUR BUSINESS IN THE RIGHT PLACE   27

RULE #7   MODEL YOUR BUSINESS AFTER THE BEST   31

RULE #8   KNOW THE DETAILS BUT DELEGATE TO TRUSTED EMPLOYEES   35

| RULE #9 | EXECUTE WITH EXCELLENCE | 37 |
| RULE #10 | MASTER THE ART OF RISK MANAGEMENT | 41 |

Part Three: Build a Winning Team   45

RULE #11	FORM A TEAM OF ADVISORS — SPOUSE, SUCCESSFUL BUSINESS FRIENDS, ACQUISITION CONSULTANT	47
RULE #12	GET THE RIGHT CFO	51
RULE #13	FIND THE BEST LAWYER	55
RULE #14	HIRING THE BEST EMPLOYEE	59
RULE #15	HIRE THE GREAT TEMP	65
RULE #16	FOSTER ENTREPRENEUR-EMPLOYEE TRUST	69
RULE #17	HOW MEN AND WOMEN DIFFER WHEN IT COMES TO TRUST AND LOYALTY	77
RULE #18	REWARD THE HARD WORKER	81

Part Four: Challenging Times   87

| RULE #19 | BE PARANOID ABOUT LOSING CUSTOMERS, EMPLOYEES, REPUTATION | 89 |

RULE #20	FIRING YOUR FIRST EMPLOYEE	93
RULE #21	THE 80% RULE	99
RULE #22	CONDUCT BACKGROUND CHECKS ON EVERY EMPLOYEE	107
RULE #23	USE MONITORING SOFTWARE	111
RULE #24	HOW TO HANDLE THE TOXIC EMPLOYEE	115
RULE #25	HOW TO DEAL WITH DIFFICULT EMPLOYEES	119
RULE #26	DON'T LET AN UNETHICAL EMPLOYEE IMPACT YOUR BUSINESS	123
RULE #27	DON'T TAKE ANY ABUSE FROM ANYONE ABOUT HOW YOU RUN YOUR BUSINESS	127
RULE #28	THINK TWICE ABOUT GIVING EQUITY TO EMPLOYEES	133
RULE #29	DON'T LET ANY EMPLOYEE HELP SELL YOUR BUSINESS – SELL IT YOURSELF	137
RULE #30	LEARN THE ART OF INTERRUPTING	141

Part Five: Growing Pains   145

RULE #31	FIND THE RIGHT CUSTOMERS	147
RULE #32	FIND CONSULTANTS WHO WILL HELP YOU, NOT HURT YOU	155

RULE #33   KNOW WHEN TO SAY NO
           TO A PIECE OF BUSINESS   161

RULE #34   DON'T LET A FEW BAD
           YEARS KILL YOUR DREAM   165

Part Six: Achieve Work-Life Balance   171

RULE #35   LIFE MOVES IN CYCLES   173

RULE #36   CLEAR YOUR HEAD BEFORE
           TAKING ON A MONSTER   177

RULE #37   SELLING YOUR BUSINESS: ON ACQUISITION-
           LEAVE IT IN GOOD SHAPE, BUT LEAVE IT 183

INTRODUCTION

In the first months, I often wondered, "What have I done?" In my early thirties, with a new baby boy at home, I'd given up a regular paycheck with job security and risked almost all my wife's and my savings to start a new company. My wife Sue and I were the only employees. Company headquarters was a small office above our garage in Cape Elizabeth, Maine.

Beyond our wildest dreams, we grew that company until it had over 250 employees, with 7 offices nationwide, and was a leader in the event marketing industry.

THE ENTREPRENEUR'S RULE BOOK

As a young CEO, I tried many new things, as my business went through growing pains. Some of them worked. Some of them didn't. *The Entrepreneur's Rule Book*, draws on my 25 years of experience as a marketing executive and CEO. I hope that it will save you time and stress by offering many lessons that I had to learn the hard way.

This book can show you what works and what doesn't in creating a successful business.

This is the type of book I wish I had when I started my business. *The Entrepreneur's Rule Book* features quick tips for typical problems that entrepreneurs face at every stage of business.

Along with a dedicated team of advisors and employees, I built Pierce Promotions into a premier marketing business before selling it for a multimillion-dollar figure to Omnicom Group, a global leader in marketing and advertising.

Corporations come in a dazzling variety. Whether you have an idea for a pizza restaurant or want to build and sell

INTRODUCTION

the next great bio-medical device, *The Entrepreneur's Rule Book* can give you proven ideas you can apply right away to take your business to the next level.

The Entrepreneur's Rule Book can change your life. It is more than a pocket guide of generalized advice, it's a blueprint – and if you follow its action steps, you too may achieve the amazing results that so many have achieved. Many who write about how to grow a business are business professors or motivational speakers who haven't done it. We've done it. We've met payroll, managed difficult employees, won our industry's highest awards, and successfully sold Pierce Promotions for every penny it was worth.

Let *The Entrepreneur's Rule Book* guide you toward your first million and, more importantly, toward living the life of which you've always dreamed.

PART ONE:

BELIEVE IN YOUR SUCCESS

RULE #1

BELIEVE IN YOURSELF

I've always been a confident guy. One snowy day in Maine, I walked out of the office building and said goodbye to my boss. "Well," I told him, "I'm going out on my own now, hoping to make my first million." A brash statement, but I believed it. Where this belief came from, I'm not sure. I came from modest means — with no family money to bail me out if I should fail. But in every fiber of my being, I believed my new business would succeed. I had an almost eerie sense of self-confidence.

THE ENTREPRENEUR'S RULE BOOK

You need to be confident, too. Having a great idea is a big help in growing a business, but having total confidence is crucial. If you're not confident, why should your employees be? All success begins with thought, and the thoughts and images in our minds create our lives. You must make up your mind to succeed at whatever you set out to do — whether it's starting a business or reaching any other goal. Then commit yourself to doing whatever it takes to succeed.

You need to be confident and to commit yourself to doing whatever it takes, because success won't come right away. Often the difference between those who make it and those who don't is pure perseverance. And perseverance is almost impossible without confidence. Thomas Edison failed 3,000 times to make an electric light bulb before he succeeded. Milton Hershey started three unsuccessful candy companies before founding the Hershey Company, which brought the Swiss delicacy of milk chocolate to the

BELIEVE IN YOUR SUCCESS

masses and made huge profits, as he knew it would. When you encounter obstacles, let Edison's words inspire you to persevere: "Many of life's failures are people who did not realize how close they were to success when they gave up."

☐ *Combine belief with action steps to reach your goal.*

RULE #2

PLAN OUT YOUR ENTIRE BUSINESS BEFORE LEAVING YOUR 9-5

Don't plan your business during work hours at your current job. It may threaten your paycheck and your good reputation, both of which are essential to you and your family. But make planning the new business the dominating focus of your free time.

Hire a first-rate attorney to draw up your corporate papers and handle any future legal problems. And find a first-rate accountant. Most new businesses lose money, but a good accountant can guide you through the financial process and become a long-standing advisor to both your business and your family. Whatever you do, don't hire under-qualified family or friends to help with legal and financial matters. Hire the best. While it may cost you more, it will be money well spent if you ever have serious litigation or financial issues.

These advisors will have been with you from the beginning, trusted allies that will have a great deal of pride when you grow and ultimately sell your company.

My single most important piece of advice to all new entrepreneurs, when planning a new business, is to purchase and learn how to use simple financial software, like QuickBooks. One of the biggest reasons new business people fail is that they just don't know how to handle money. You need a good accountant to help you file taxes and understand legal financial obligations, but it's up to you to manage the day-to-day financials of your business, especially in the first few years of operation.

BELIEVE IN YOUR SUCCESS

Don't ever say, "I'm not good at the money thing." That's a very bad sign for your business. From the first day of being in business to the last day in my role as CEO of the company I sold, I was always involved with the dollars to make sure we were being profitable and money was not being wasted.

To minimize the risk of losing a steady paycheck, before you leave your job, try and save enough money to cover your personal expenses for a minimum of 6 months. In my case, my wife Sue and I had a mortgage to pay and a baby at home, so it was important to be able to cover those bills and not lose everything. You just don't need that stress. You will have enough just getting your business started.

I recommend you plan your new business venture over a 6-12 month period prior to leaving your full-time job. So many people just want to make the jump as fast as possible and in my opinion, you increase your failure rate that much more. Here are a few other things you can do to plan before leaving your 9-5:

- Only share your plans with your spouse/significant other, attorney, and accountant. Make sure they clearly understand that everything is confidential. Have your attorney and accountant sign an agreement confirming their pledge of confidentiality. The last thing you want is to have a great idea picked up by someone else. Don't tell friends and neighbors about your plans — and especially not co-workers!
- Determine with a confidential attorney and accountant if you should be an S-Corp or an LLC.
- Test your accounting software over and over again, and make sure you understand budgeting.
- Write up a business plan that includes personal goals.
- Get great business insurance coverage.
- Create a corporate budget with all potential revenues, expenses, and expected profits.

BELIEVE IN YOUR SUCCESS

- Create a customer target list.
- Discuss with your attorney any non-compete issues that could relate to your current employer.
- Purchase basic equipment like computers, copiers, phones, etc.
- Secure Internet domain names for your website.
- If you need a space for your business, do research without letting people know you are the one starting the business. Get a confidential advisor, like your accountant or spouse, to do the negotiations.

Bottom line....be ready to open the doors of your new business the day you leave your job. You can't afford a lot of down time. You had all that time to plan and still get a regular paycheck, so don't let your ego get the best of you and push you away from security before you are ready to make the jump.

Give plenty of notice and don't burn any bridges when you leave your employer! Often, an ex-employer later becomes a client. Leaving in a classy way pays off in the future. My experience working for a wonderful marketing and communications company in Maine helped me 10 years later when we were in a major growth mode and had outgrown our space. My old employer leased to me, within a matter of days, an entire floor in his building, completely outfitted with furniture and office equipment. People who burn bridges always come to regret it. If you have burned a bridge, learn from your mistake and never do it again.

☐ ***Plan all aspects of your new business over 6-12 months and be ready to open the doors when you finally leave your 9-5.***

RULE #3

ENVISION YOUR SUCCESS

Dream about your business and all of its possibilities. What will it look like in year one and year 10? How many customers and employees will you have? Will you have one location or 100? How big will your corporate headquarters be?

It's very important to define "ultimate success" for yourself. It's also important to visualize all of this very specifically. Make a precise mental picture of it and keep it in your mind. Also, look at your company budget and financial goals several times a week. Having a very specific goal gives you something to labor toward — and makes it harder to sell yourself short.

For me, ultimate success meant founding a company that I could sell for millions of dollars. That required building a strong infrastructure of first-rate people, office space, and technology. It meant growing the company, advertising well, having an Internet presence, attracting high-profile clients, participating in industry events, and winning the highest awards.

Do everything you can to have a cool work environment. Lavish isn't necessary, but your offices, especially your entrance, should be memorably arranged and decorated, with some edge, so that they make a striking first impression. My business was located in the Old Port, on the waterfront, in Portland, Maine, a tourist environment with restaurants and cobblestone streets. Eventually, we

BELIEVE IN YOUR SUCCESS

had offices in New York City, L.A., Chicago, Washington, D.C., Bentonville, Arkansas — home of Wal-Mart — and Boston. These offices weren't fancy but they presented a professional image. I had a standing joke with some people in one office who felt I was too frugal with equipment. "When are we going to get a good copier?" they'd ask. And I would tell them "When this one breaks and can't print any longer."

Sure, they would have liked a top-of-the-line copier. They ultimately got a refurbished version that met their needs. But I think they saw that I knew how to grow a business, and was planning things much bigger than a new copier. We kept thinking up new services to offer our clients. It was exciting and created a certain momentum, and I think my employees thrived on that sense of excitement.

I even dreamed about eventually hiring my replacement. And when the time was right, I did just that.

☐ *Dream of your business very specifically, defining ultimate success for yourself — and then create the business that fulfills that dream.*

PART TWO:

HAVE A GAME PLAN

RULE #4

WRITE A SIMPLE BUSINESS PLAN

A major misconception among aspiring business owners is that a good business plan must be long and complicated and written by someone with a Masters Degree in Business Administration. If you've saved enough money to start your business without any angel investors, don't waste months crafting a 50-page business plan. Outline your goals and objectives in a simple five-page plan that you keep as your own personal guideline. You should do this in the planning phase prior to leaving your 9-5 job.

Use the plan to implement your goals for the business. Remember, you own the business and it's your plan. Don't share it with your employees. When you have grown your business to the point where it's generating significant revenue, you can then implement a more sophisticated plan that meets the needs of your employees and customers.

For year one, your business plan should include short-term goals, action steps, and a basic operating plan. You must think deeply — and realistically — about these subjects, but the business plan itself can be as short as five pages. The plan really should be looked at as your own, "personal" plan for business. Personal goals tie in very closely with your business goals, and you will find, by doing this, you will have a much more balanced family life during those crazy first few years of owning the business.

Here are a few other items you will want to include in the plan:

HAVE A GAME PLAN

- Where and how will you get customers.
- Who are your main competitors.
- Financial goals for your business in year one, including your salary and company profit.
- What major purchases do you plan to make for the company (e.g. technology, office space, website development, equipment, business travel)
- How many employees you intend to hire.

Make a habit of updating your plan every New Year's Day and checking off what you accomplished from the previous year. I felt a great deal of satisfaction doing this every New Year's. I made sure I reached my goals from both a business and personal standpoint. I included things like "Hire 10 more employees" or "Add 3 more clients" or "Take family vacations every holiday" in order to have quality family time, "Stay in shape by working out five days a week" and even "Save enough money to buy a new house."

I really enjoyed updating the plan, checking off my accomplishments and creating new goals every New Year's Day. I would always say to my wife, "Can you believe we did all this?" You will be surprised how successful you can be with a simple plan.

☐ *Create a simple business plan that includes both business and personal goals.*

RULE #5

THE NO DEBT ENTREPRENEUR

The first thing out of most entrepreneurs' mouths is: "Where am I going to get the money to start my business?" And the best answer is: "You and your partner should save that start-up money right out of the salaries from your current jobs." And if you can't save enough to get the doors open, you better think long and hard about whether you're really up to starting a business at all.

A business needs to grow — but it doesn't need to grow fast. Entrepreneurs who choose to "make a splash" by quickly opening multiple locations or hiring a ton of people rarely survive. That kind of spending leads to major debt, and that kind of debt brings you stress, limits your options, and makes your business look a lot less appealing to potential buyers.

Anytime you're tempted to borrow money, imagine asking the banker or investor: "Would you like control over me, my company and what I do?" If it feels awkward to ask that question, it's going to feel ten times worse when it's reality.

So how do you grow your business without taking on debt? You plan, you get strong financial management and you do a lot of the work yourself instead of using expensive vendors. Websites, for example. Only a fool pays a boutique website designer $50,000 for a "state-of-the-art" site. Design your own website on your own time. Cheap software will show you how or use a low cost on-line domain name and web business.

Get yourself a line of credit with the bank to help with billing and revenue timing issues. But pay it off every

HAVE A GAME PLAN

month, and stay out of debt to the bank. Just because the bank is happy to accept a monthly minimum payment doesn't mean that's the way to go.

In the early days of your company, profit margins will be small, and motivation of your employees will be crucial. Sit your employees down once a week and give them "The Talk." You can vary it with jokes, or good news about a new customer, but the heart of your message should never change: "This company is going places. Right now, your desks and desk chairs are second-hand, but that's because we're investing and staying financially stable, in order to grow."

It will grow, and eventually you will sell — and if you've avoided relying on banks and investors, the whole check will be yours.

☐ *Be frugal from the start, and take your big payday at the end.*

RULE #6

PUT YOUR BUSINESS IN THE RIGHT PLACE

Business success depends on a good location. If possible, look for a low-cost city, paying special attention to local rates in office leasing, utilities, wages, and business taxes. Successfully expanding your business will be much easier with low overhead.

You don't need to be based in a "major" city, a big market — but, to grow significantly, you need great air service between your city and major markets.

THE ENTREPRENEUR'S RULE BOOK

Quality-of-life is important, too. It will help you attract and retain highly qualified workers, without overpaying for them.

Portland, Maine, for example, was a perfect location to base our business. It has a plentiful workforce with an easy two-hour drive to Boston and a one-hour flight to New York. Portland has a beautiful Old Port section that our customers liked to visit. It has great restaurants nearby to entertain clients and an airport just ten minutes from downtown.

Finding the right location within a city is critical. Do your research and find the location that makes the most sense for your customer base. Don't just jump into the first space you find because it's priced right. You are committing generally for at least a year, if not three or five, so make sure there's room to grow and that you'll enjoy being in the location.

HAVE A GAME PLAN

Being in Portland's Old Port was a real perk for our employees, and it made a big difference in their daily life. If they were having a bad day, they could always go out into the Old Port for a nice lunch or walk and come back with a fresh perspective.

It's always good to find a place that you don't have to commit to for any long period of time. In your first few years of business you will need a great deal of flexibility, so make sure you don't just sign on the dotted line. Negotiate what makes sense for you and your business, and always keep your eyes open for future space that will allow you to grow your business.

☐ *Find a location for your business that will help it thrive.*

RULE #7

MODEL YOUR BUSINESS AFTER THE BEST

No matter what your business, you have rivals. Study and learn from them. Industry leaders don't get there by accident; they are examples of success, and you can find and leverage those successes for your own business.

Study the second-rate firms, too. Dissect their performance and see what they're doing wrong. In business, it's okay to learn from your mistakes — but it's much better to learn from someone else's mistakes.

THE ENTREPRENEUR'S RULE BOOK

Very few event marketing companies existed in the 1990's when we started our business. So I looked to businesses in other industries that I knew were well run. Fortunately, I had worked for an entrepreneurial company with outstanding management and systems and before that had worked for a large corporation with the same type of DNA.

Whenever you're at work, closely follow how great companies operate. Trust your instincts, but also analyze what works and what doesn't. Take mental notes and ask yourself a lot of questions.

When you open your doors and in the first few years of business, follow the industry award winners. Watch how effectively they control how they are perceived by others. Watch who acquires their business. It was one of our key competitors, also purchased by

HAVE A GAME PLAN

Omnicom Group, that recommended Omnicom acquire our company.

☐ *Model your company on the biggest, most respected players in your industry.*

RULE #8

KNOW THE DETAILS BUT DELEGATE TO EMPLOYEES

Details are everything in a business. Attention to detail is what distinguishes good from great companies, and it's what drives customer loyalty, too. Therefore, your employees need to learn attention to detail in their first few months of employment and to demonstrate it daily on the job.

Giving the Meyers-Briggs or similar personality tests to potential employees can be very helpful. If your organization requires extensive detail work, then you should probably work with a HR consultant who understands how to test for that capability. Attention to detail must be in the very DNA of your company.

But that doesn't mean you have to be a micromanager. If you choose the right people to work for you, give them the right hands-on training, and use meetings and communication systems to monitor events and job performance, then your company can thrive. Promote hard-working top-tier employees whom you can trust to carry out your vision.

To be creative and successful, an organization needs all types of people. However, a great idea is worth nothing unless it's well-executed. You may always be looking for that next great idea. But, before you put the product or service in front of your customers, make sure you can deliver.

☐ *Handpick detail-oriented, trusted employees to run key areas of your business.*

RULE #9

EXECUTE WITH EXCELLENCE

Wanting your company to be excellent is not enough. You must be *obsessed* with delivering excellent products and services. Well-written training manuals are a good start. But senior staff should constantly reinforce the message, both in word and deed, that excellence is essential.

"Execute with Excellence." Make that phrase your company mantra — not only in your marketing materials and presentations to clients, but in conversations with colleagues, and in the daily life of your company. Only hire and promote people who see a great responsibility in their work with customers.

Sweat the details. We staged major events for Fortune 500 companies, at the Super Bowl, in the Macy's Day Parade, and at major concert venues. For all of those events, there were a myriad of details we had to handle in a professional manner. It was a grind, but it was all worth it, because our attention to detail made the events run smoothly. And our clients noticed.

In every part of your business details are everything— hiring, financial, creative — so be smart! Don't just do things a certain way because "everyone else does." Is there a better model?

When someone in the company makes a mistake, make it a "teachable moment." Explain clearly, but without scorn, exactly what went wrong, and why. Then solicit ideas from those involved, and from their supervisors, about how to ensure the mistake won't happen again. If the process

HAVE A GAME PLAN

produces two different ideas and both of them are good, adopt them both! You'll have multiple systems in place to prevent such mistakes — and two different employees proud of having solved the problem.

When a customer makes a special request of your company, don't reply "We'll see what we can do..." The response must be: "Let's get that done!" Because any customer's problem is your problem. The customers most loyal to a company are not those who've never had a problem with the company. The most loyal customers are those who have had a problem — but seen the company fix it, promptly, and in style.

Sometimes crisis is an opportunity. One day, a mini-tornado ripped through one of our parking lot events at a major retailer. A huge tent, well-anchored to the ground, was blown right out of the parking lot. But our staff kept its poise and we had systems in place in case of bad weather. We confirmed with weather professionals that the most

severe weather had passed. We quickly reset the event —
including a new tent — and the event was a success. The
crisis of the tornado gave us the chance to show our client
how committed we were to their success.

Impressed, that company gave us more work.

☐ *Excellent execution is essential — and crisis can be an opportunity.*

RULE #10

MASTER THE ART OF RISK MANAGEMENT

When my wife and I first started the business, we endured some very stressful moments and sleepless nights. We were fortunate to have very large corporations as customers from the start. The event marketing industry was in its infancy and we got in on the ground floor. We knew that every event had to go perfectly, so I started holding Risk Management Meetings - brainstorming sessions to discuss everything that could go wrong at an event. We discussed all elements of the event that included potential staffing issues, timing of set up, customer meetings on site, permitting, insurance, etc. I learned about Risk Management Meetings from a previous employer and very early on saw all the benefits.

These types of meetings are worth every minute because by discussing everything that could go wrong and putting contingencies in place, you can create a situation where everything goes right! No matter what type of business you have, discuss all the risks on a regular basis and plan how to deal with them. You might not hit every one of the risks in your first few years of holding these types of meetings, but you will hit almost 90%. The other 10% of the time you will learn from your mistakes and hopefully still end up with an A rating from your customers.

Risk Management Meetings are also a very good time for the entrepreneur to get to know if people are doing their job well. If they have planned for the potential problems, then you know they are doing their job. It's impossible to

HAVE A GAME PLAN

sit in on all meetings as your business grows, but if I had one word of advice, it's to sit in on these meetings because you as the owner have experienced everything that can go wrong and can advise your staff even at the last minute on how to improve something. These types of meetings are an opportunity for you to tell some funny war stories that everyone will remember and learn from. Those stories are memorable and will help your employees understand that you are just like them and can make mistakes, but still be very successful in business.

☐ *Brainstorm everything that might go wrong and create a contingency plan to match.*

PART THREE:

BUILD A WINNING TEAM

RULE #11

FORM A STRONG TEAM OF ADVISORS

No entrepreneur knows everything and, as a leader, admitting that you need help in certain areas is not a weakness, but a strength. Many CEOs of Fortune 500 companies have used an executive coach from time to time. Secure in their own skins, they know there are still more things to learn, and that a coach can help. Seek out gifted lawyers, accountants and business owners, especially those who have bought and sold a business. Pick their brains.

You will need an excellent acquisition specialist since being acquired, or not, can mean a difference of millions of dollars. You may be in touch with this specialist for years before the sale of your company goes through. This person should be someone you can talk to about anything, has a strong reputation, communicates aggressively and knows how to get the job done. No matter what, make sure they have done a lot of deals in your business sector.

Never underestimate the wisdom of your own spouse. They know you better than anyone else. They know your strengths and weaknesses, they can sense abnormal tension and stress in you — and they have good instincts about which solutions will fit your skills and temperament.

Ideally, your closest advisor will be your spouse or another close family member. You want your closest advisor to be a person you can trust with confidential information, and someone with something to lose if you go out of business. While your spouse may not be actively involved in the daily operations of your firm, they can be a great sounding board at the kitchen table at night.

Because the talks you give at the office should be relentlessly upbeat, you will need someone with whom you can unburden yourself about things at work, someone who will patiently listen as you vent your anger and frustration, share your doubts and concerns — and with total confidence that all of this will *stay* in confidence. Because running your business will be such a consuming passion in your life, try to bring your spouse into the process, solicit their advice, assign them special projects, perhaps even put them on the payroll.

Lawyers, accountants, close business friends, acquisitions specialists, spouse...These people are your unofficial Board of Directors/your personal Advisory Council. They need not all like each other, nor even know each other. They don't have to meet with you as a group. But their skills and interests should complement one another, and all of them should be confidential.

☐ *Create your own unofficial Board of Directors/ personal Advisory Council to help guide you in the right direction.*

RULE #12

GET THE RIGHT CFO

I discuss throughout this book the importance of being a good financial manager and having advisors and employees with a similar focus. When your business reaches a certain level in terms of revenue and employees, you will need an expert to handle a wide variety of tax and compliance issues for your business. This is your Chief Financial Officer (CFO).

Many business owners start out with an Accounting Manager or Business Manager as their first real financial managers. While these people can be critical to the growth of your business and help you many times when the business is in its infancy, there is no substitute for someone who is a Certified Public Accountant (CPA) and has worked either for a large accounting firm or in a high-level capacity at another business. Having experience with both is most ideal.

Trust is key in the CFO position and you need to be sure this person will be totally confidential with your business operations and finances. You own the business and it's not anyone's business how you choose to run it, or how much money you make, so keep profits confidential.

One of the biggest mistakes entrepreneurs make is letting employees know the numbers. This doesn't help anyone, as most employees never have the entire picture, including expenses, your own personal investment and the overall risk of owning the business. So never share these numbers with anyone other than your CFO, your accountant, and your spouse. There can be hard feelings if you start sharing the financial picture in a good year and then have a bad year and have to put money into infrastructure and choose not to make a profit. Employees might misread this as an unstable work environment, and then you might lose key people.

Hire the best financial people possible, pay them well, and require total confidentiality. Most CPA's have it in their DNA to be confidential, but interview them at length to be sure of this and also be sure they come with excellent credentials. Having the right CFO is one of the greatest determinants of your future success or failure.

☐ *Even a financially gifted CEO needs a first-rate and confidential Chief Financial Officer.*

RULE #13

FIND THE BEST ATTORNEY

People who use friends or family as their company's first attorney almost always regret it. As your business expands, you'll need a large law firm. It's awkward, at best, to fire a family member or old friend as your attorney. At worst, it can cause a permanent rift in your family or friendship. But remaining loyal to an underqualified attorney puts your company needlessly at risk.

Does it "feel good" to throw some legal business to a family member? Sure it does. But it also feels good to sit in a $1,000 chair — and you don't do that, either. Especially in the early years, when your business is vulnerable, every decision must be based on whether or not it's good for your business. Using a law firm that doesn't specialize in what you need is never good for your business.

A large, expensive, diversified law firm will ultimately save your business money. Great law firms don't win lawsuits; they prevent lawsuits from ever being filed by anticipating areas of legal risk.

Do your research, and find a large law firm that's highly regarded in the business world and in your community. The firm should handle business law, employment law, liability, government relations, real estate, patent law, litigation, copyright, trademark law — everything. And don't let yourself get assigned some young hot shot attorney. The older the better, with years of experience under their belt and great relationships with the courts.

BUILD A WINNING TEAM

Keep your business law firm separate from your family firm. Keep issues like trusts and family taxes separate, because when you sell your business, your business law firm cannot represent you if they're hired on by the new company, post sale.

Speaking of selling your business, that's another time when you need a legal specialist. In my case, my acquisition advisor recommended several law firms that had done many deals in the industry, and ultimately saved us thousands of dollars. Never use a law firm that has not completed acquisitions in your industry.

☐ *Legal work and family friends don't mix. Hire a large, well-known law firm, of wide expertise, right from the start.*

RULE #14

HIRING THE BEST EMPLOYEE

Defining the "best" employee is no easy task. Those you think are the best one day, could become the worst a month later. People are people, and it's up to you to motivate them and give them a lot of support, allowing them to excel at their job.

Hiring your first employee will be one of your most challenging moments. You won't want to make any mistakes in the process, but you probably will. How much money you have budgeted for salaries will be a major factor in how your business turns out. Can you pay a decent wage? You want to pay people well, but you also want a hungry, hard-working staff. Be clear with them: "This is a start up business and, as the owner, I still have a lot to learn about running my own company. But, if all goes well, you have a chance to be in on the ground floor of something great."

You will need to be very clear with the first hires, that you may need them to do just about anything to help support the business, including flying off to a meeting at the last minute or running to make the last FedEx drop at 7 pm. Interview at length and find out the applicant's likes and dislikes, their tolerance for last-minute adjustments, and their interest in being a loyal member of a team.

Whatever you do, don't hire someone who is just looking for a 9-5 job. If they came from a business that worked 9-5 and you find this out in the interview process, don't even consider the person. There's nothing worse than hiring a person with a 9-5 mentality when you're trying to meet a daily deadline, and you ask the person to stay late for work, and they say, "Sorry, I have to go to the gym for my spin class." or "Sorry, I have to meet my friends at the bar down the street."

While I'm a huge believer in staying healthy and having fun with friends after work, you can't afford to have employees who take off in the middle of something. So no matter what, be clear about what your business is like and what you'll expect of each employee.

Get the hire right by doing your homework. Let's say you have an applicant come to you with great credentials. If overnight travel is a requirement for the job and the person tells you they don't like to travel, then don't hire them — even if they have great credentials. If you hire them, you and your other employees will end up traveling for them and end up with a resentful relationship. This may sound like a simple concept, but I made that mistake and learned the hard way. We ultimately parted ways.

So make sure the applicant fits your needs, no matter what. As your business grows, you can become a little more flexible but, in the first few years, flexibility is something that the employees give to the company — not the other way around.

I was blessed with wonderful employees from the start. Try to start out by hiring people who will look to you as a mentor. Don't be afraid to hire someone right out of college. They will be so grateful that you hired them. You will get an incredible amount of work out of them — and also avoid having to pay the high salary that a more experienced person might require.

Experience and education are less important in your employees than energy, dedication, smarts, and a work ethic. Four out of five of the people I hired were either right out of college, had five years or less experience, or came to us as a temp. Several did not have college degrees, but came with great experience. Don't rule out a person just because they don't have a degree. You could really miss out on someone great.

There's a saying I would always use: "Hire smart, nice people," and we did just that. I made this the mission of our Human Resource Department and, from the start, this was what made our company great. We had smart people who could think fast on their feet, and nice people who got along well with others, showed respect and truly cared about their co-workers.

You really don't want a lot of aggressive, mean-spirited people anywhere in your life, but the entrepreneur can't afford to have those types of people around at all. The occasional bully would somehow make it through our interview process — and when they came on board, they'd upset the entire culture I was trying to create.

In the reference check process, listen carefully. If people use phrases like "really quick," "detailed," "nice," "fun to be with," and "will be missed by everyone," then you know you have a good candidate. If they don't use these types of words — beware of what you could be getting yourself into.

You will also get incredible satisfaction seeing your employees grow into great managers and leaders in your organization. Even if they leave, they will always remember how much they learned from you and your company. I'm very proud that there are people who learned the business, in my company, who are now throughout the country leading other organizations, and even growing their own companies.

Be proud of founding a business. You might not be saving the world, but you are providing jobs to your community, giving people a chance to grow and maybe, in some small way, even helping an individual go off on their own to create another great company.

☐ *Hire smart, nice people.*

RULE #15

HIRE THE GREAT TEMP

One of the best ways to deal with growth in your company is to hire temporary workers. Build a close relationship with a few good temporary employment agencies in your city. Give them the specifics of the job and the type of person you're looking for. Using temp agencies allows you great flexibility, as your business grows and goes through busier periods.

You should do a quick interview of each temp, before they start work, just to get a feeling for his or her professional skills. But a good temp agency will have done all the primary interviewing and background checks.

There's no better way to evaluate a worker than to watch them on the job. Using temps allows you to try out a person, with no strings attached, before deciding whether or not to hire them permanently. You can quickly get rid of those who don't meet the job requirements, and there's no emotional mess about the firings because you pay the temp agencies to handle all that. The bad temp gets paid his wages, and simply doesn't come back.

Some temps will be really great and come with very good experience. Try them out for a few months to get to know them. If someone is really good, a manager will come to you and say, "We need to hire this person right away." Then hire the temp as a permanent employee.

Temp agencies generally charge a modest fee when you hire people on permanently. But paying the fee is well

BUILD A WINNING TEAM

worth it. Or you can negotiate a deal where you pay no fee to hire a temp permanently, so long as the temp has worked for you for a few months and the agency has received good compensation through their cut of the temp's hourly rate.

Most temps are eager to do a great job, as most are looking for a full-time job. When you end up hiring one of them, they are very appreciative and can become some of your top performers. The majority of my hires, in the first 10 years of my business, were people who came to my company as temporary workers.

☐ *Find a good temporary agency in your town and then hire the great temp as a permanent employee.*

RULE #16

FOSTER ENTREPRENEUR-EMPLOYEE TRUST

Why Trust Matters

Finding trustworthy employees and building trust with your employees and customers is critical to an entrepreneur's success. Trust is one of the hottest research topics in business schools today. Research is proving what wise employers have always known — that establishing and maintaining trust between employee and entrepreneur is critical to success. High trust organizations run efficiently.

Trusting and being trustworthy are two sides of the same coin. To a business owner, trust is essential because he or she depends on employees to run key business operations, to represent them to important customers, and to handle sensitive financial information. The company's whole success depends on the integrity of the employees, and so does the owner's reputation. Entrepreneurs must trust their employees to execute their jobs well, without much oversight.

Employees, in turn, depend on their employer for satisfying work, a steady income, a safe, interesting work environment, and advancement in their field. If the employee has dependents, the employee relies on the employer even more.

Below are some tips for determining how much you can trust employees and potential employers:

Look for employees who possess integrity and competence. They will be the most trustworthy.

Seek out employees who grasp the importance of fiscal responsibility. In my business, they were the ones who always rose to the occasion, helping me whenever we faced a challenge.

Trustworthiness (of entrepreneur and employee) is a partnership earned, over two years or more, by following through on promises, and meeting the expectations of the partner.

Set an expectation of fair treatment. Persons with integrity don't exploit other people's weaknesses, and an entrepreneur and his or her employees must prove they won't take unfair advantage of each other's vulnerabilities.

Take steps to determine the competence, willingness, and ethical behavior of those who work for you. If you trust blindly and are taken advantage of, then you have brought the problem on yourself. The trustor must conduct due diligence to determine how trustworthy is the trusted party. And the trusted party must make full disclosure.

Be careful about whom you can trust, to what extent, and in what capacity. When trust is betrayed, it can be painful to the individuals and ruinous to the company. "Who can I trust?" "How much?" "Under what circumstances?"

Keeps confidential information confidential. Trusted employees never pass on confidential information. If your confidence is broken once, reconsider your relationship with the employee, their commitment to you, and to the company. If it happens a second time, quietly but firmly, usher them out of the company.

Make sure employees let you know when they need more help on a project. Sometimes what looks like disloyalty is really the desperate move of a good person who needs help.

Tips for Building Trust

Be clear in your expectations. State your expectations clearly to each other. Trusting your employees often elicits trustworthy behavior in them. But make clear that you will not be exploited.

Give a little trust, then assess. Was your expectation or desired outcome achieved? Did you trust too much, or too little? Adjust your behavior accordingly.

Implement a six-month training period, even for senior hires. I did not trust employees to send out important client documents until they were completely proofed by a trusted supervisor or me. Train your employees to have all the skills they will need to work for you. It's shocking how many people cannot write a professional business document. You simply cannot hand over important work to new employees, no matter how senior, and think they will perform according to your company culture.

Value employees who understand it's your business. Trust employees who say things like "You started this business, you own it, and you take all the risks. You should be able to run it your way." Employees who sharply question how you're running the business are rarely a good fit.

Care for each other. Employees care about how well they are treated as people. So do entrepreneurs.

Take every new employee to lunch. This is a great way to get to know him or her and to build trust. Even if you have hundreds of employees, try to have a one-on-one with each employee. It really shows an employee that the leader of the business knows and cares about him. You will also discover useful information in the one-on-one meetings about the person's background, motivation, and insights into the workings of their department.

Paying employees well is critical to building trust and loyalty. While we didn't have the nicest furniture, we always paid people well. Although they worked long hours, the whole time I owned the business, my employees always knew they were well paid — and nothing is more key to building trust.

BUILD A WINNING TEAM

Offer great benefits. Try to offer great medical benefits to your employees right from the start. The cost is outrageous, but it's crucial to attracting and keeping good people. Forget fancy furniture and expensive equipment — put your money into compensation and benefits. If you offer above average market compensation and if you truly care about your people, they will come to trust you and believe in you, and your business will be much more likely to succeed.

The Real Purpose of Trust

For entrepreneurs, a trusting relationship with a business colleague is very gratifying. Over the years, you work toward a common goal, support each other in tough times, and celebrate the good times. With luck, the business relationship becomes a lasting, meaningful friendship.

As entrepreneurs, we will be remembered not only by how much money our company made, but by how we treated people, how much we cared, and how much others cared for us. In the life of a business, there is nothing more inspiring than showing a firm faith in the ability, integrity, and character of those with whom we work. And there is nothing more crucial to our success.

☐ *Hire employees who exhibit integrity, kindness, and competence.*

RULE #17

HOW MEN AND WOMEN DIFFER WHEN IT COMES TO TRUST AND LOYALTY

I can't give you scientific research on the subject, but I know from experience that women are more likely than men to stick with an entrepreneurial boss during tough times. A number of factors may contribute to this. In smaller entrepreneurial businesses, women have a chance to rise much more quickly into key positions of leadership, than their female counterparts do in the corporate world.

The compensation gap can be much greater in large corporations versus small.

My wife and I ran our company together until we had our fourth child. While working together can put a real strain on a relationship, my wife's high level of expertise made for a very successful and balanced work environment. The men and women who worked for her looked up to her and trusted her ability to make good decisions and to come through with solutions when the going got tough.

Though men are trusted in business, women are more trusted. A ***Management Today*** **poll states:** "Overall trust in female CEOs remains higher than trust in male CEOs, as was the case in 2010. The largest year-on-year increase in CEO trust is experienced between male employees and their female CEOs — an increase of eight index points. And most of this increasing level of trust was experienced by non-managers, who registered an increase of a massive

BUILD A WINNING TEAM

11 index points in their trust for their female CEO between 2009 and 2010.

What has fueled this rise? Women rate more highly than their male counterparts both when it comes to employees having confidence in their boss's ability to do their job and also when it comes to being principled and honest. Female CEOs score higher than male CEOs in these areas by two and three index points respectively.

But the really important differentiator is chief executives' knowledge of what their employees have to contend with in their day-to-day lives — female CEOs are seven points ahead of their male counterparts on this measure. When times are tough, it helps to at least know that your chief executive understands your predicament, even if he or she can't do much about it."

Turnover can be higher among men in some entrepreneurial businesses. Men are much more likely to jump ship for that next job — forcing their old business to spend valuable time searching for an adequate successor.

In my company, about 60% of my employees were women. I promoted women to key roles as Chief Financial Officer (CFO), Chief Marketing Officer (CMO) and Chief Creative Officer (CCO). These people were part of my inner circle. I could always count on them for complete confidentiality.

I would always promote a loyal person, who had our best interest in mind, over someone slightly more qualified, but less loyal. I recommend you do the same. It's the loyal and trustworthy employees who make a business thrive. They keep a close eye on details, and on other workers, ensuring your company culture is thriving.

☐ *Hire and promote women into key positions requiring high levels of trust and loyalty.*

RULE #18

REWARD THE HARD WORKER

Everyone works harder when they know hard work gets rewarded. You have many options at your disposal to reward the hard worker. I would give employees gift certificates for two at a top restaurant or send someone to an inn for a weekend with their spouse. Once, I even hired a carpenter to fix the roof on someone's house.

Employees love these types of rewards and are always very appreciative. They might say, "You didn't have to do this," or sometimes break down crying because they're so appreciative that you noticed their efforts. You and your department heads will get a great deal of satisfaction giving out these types of rewards. While they may not be thousands of dollars, and I did that, too, they will be well deserved and help build a loyal relationship between you and your employees.

Large discretionary bonuses are also critical for the success of an entrepreneurial business. Giving a sizable bonus ($1,000-$5,000) for the completion of a major project, the opening of a new division, or staying within budget on a multi-million dollar deal motivates people. Letting your employees know the logistics of how bonuses will work gives them a great financial incentive to reach a goal on time and within budget.

Throughout the life of your business, you are going to have a slew of projects you will need completed. It could be implementing the newest financial software, converting the company from PC to Mac, writing your first employee

BUILD A WINNING TEAM

manual, or coordinating the move to a new headquarters. Although you can handle some of these projects yourself, many will need to be delegated to trusted employees. This gives you time to focus on big picture plans for the future. Motivation is essential for your employees to effectively and efficiently complete these projects. Words are one thing, but money is something that employees bring home to their families with great pride. These types of bonuses and rewards are critical to your business growth and survival.

As your business grows, plan out a number you will use for rewards and discretionary bonuses throughout the year. If you are having a great year and can afford it, modify that number as needed and add a few more projects and bonuses that will take your business to the next level.

Holding regular parties and celebrations for your staff and their spouses is a great way to raise moral and promote unity among your staff. When I started my company, we celebrated everything. The largest celebration was a yearly holiday party that employees looked forward to all year. We put bottles of champagne on every desk with flags to celebrate the Fourth of July, put candy on every desk for Valentine's Day, had costume contests on holidays, and as a company, donated thousands of dollars in toys and gifts every holiday season.

Small, spontaneous rewards help make the workplace a more fun environment and build a relationship between you and your employees. When I was running my company, if we won a large customer account or major industry award, I would take the entire company out for dinner or drinks and appetizers to celebrate. The staff and I loved doing this, and it made the work environment more fun. When you work as hard as everyone does in an entrepreneurial business, people need to relax and celebrate a job well done every once and a while. Celebrations and rewards make your business unique and maintain strong employee morale. It makes your job a lot more fun, too!

☐ *Make your business fun, give rewards, and celebrate.*

PART FOUR:

CHALLENGING TIMES

RULE #19

BE PARANOID ABOUT LOSING CUSTOMERS, EMPLOYEES, REPUTATION

When I was running my company, my wife would always say: "You're so paranoid!" She was teasing me, but in a way it's true. Why should I assume today's going to go well just because yesterday did? Why should I trust all of my employees to say or do the right thing, just because they're supposed to?

I'm the sort of person that, before trouble comes, I enjoy thinking: "What could go wrong and how would I handle it?" I actually enjoy that. And if you're starting a business, I suggest you try to enjoy being paranoid, too. Because when you own a business, paranoia is good and complacency can be disastrous.

Losing a high revenue-producing customer can be devastating to your business. It can cause pay cuts and layoffs and loss of benefits. BE PARANOID! You know the impact of losing customers, so don't let it happen. If you have even the slightest sense your customer is not happy, get involved. Don't put it off. Don't wait for the perfect solution to present itself. Get the customer on the phone, and tell him: "Look, I heard about this, and I feel awful. This is how we plan to fix it."

Always keep your eyes and ears open, and look and listen for trouble. As your company grows, monitor what's happening with regular meetings and strong reporting. Keep an open door so that employees can come to you directly with a problem or a concern. Have

CHALLENGING TIMES

your employees blind copy you on client e-mails, so you stay up-to-date on customer activities. Use computer monitoring software to track all communications and activity. Use any technical tool at your disposal to gather information.

You know something else to be paranoid about? Losing great employees. These are the people who drive your business. You can sense when they're looking for another job. Little hints, sour remarks about the business, longer lunch breaks. Stay close to your top performers and figure out how to help them grow and move to the next level — without leaving your company. I rarely lost an employee who was critical to the business. Even if a top employee resigned for a new position and I wanted them to stay, I would always give a counteroffer and discuss what we could do to keep them.

The thing to be most paranoid about is your company's reputation. If you lose that, you can lose everything: your customers, your chance to grow the company, and to get it sold for a good price. Whether it's firing a bad employee who threatens your reputation or dealing with a competitor who's ruthless, always try and control the message to clients and employees. Remember, your reputation is everything.

Consistent excellence is enough for everyone except the owner of the business. The owner has to be consistently excellent — and a little paranoid, too.

☐ *Paranoia is good — and complacency is disastrous.*

RULE #20

FIRING YOUR FIRST EMPLOYEE

Firing your first employee is even more memorable than hiring your first employee. Firing someone in the small office of a business which you've founded is stressful and complicated and like nothing you have ever done before.

Don't worry too much, though, because firing people gets a lot easier as your business grows. You will learn from your mistakes, and HR specialists will make that part of your life a lot easier.

How are you going to feel about your first termination? You may feel mad at the employee for not meeting your high standards. But, most likely, you didn't do your homework and should never have hired them to begin with. You feel mad because you realize much of the failure is on your part.

It gets complicated if the employee really tries to do a good job, but is just not cutting it. If they're a really nice person, you'll feel even worse about firing them, and you may be tempted to hold onto them. Don't do that; it may soothe your conscience in the short-run but in the long-run, it will cost you money and productivity. Remember that your employee will be happier when they find a job which is a better fit. Make up your mind to do it, fire them with as much grace as you can, and then go out and get yourself a great replacement.

Oh, and be prepared to bring a box of tissues when you fire someone because, man or woman, people cry in terminations and get very emotional. Strong emotions

CHALLENGING TIMES

are perfectly all right in this situation and it may even be healthy to express them — but tears and strong emotions can have absolutely no effect on your decision. And because all the emotion can confuse people, be very clear with your fired employee that, "We are terminating your employment with us, and today is your last day."

They may groan or burst into tears and say: "Why?" But you don't have to give a lot of reasons why. If you've done your managing properly, you've already spoken with a HR consultant and your law firm, and you have given this employee several warnings, over a period of weeks or months, about their job performance and the likelihood that it will lead to a termination.

If so, your employee has been prepared for this outcome and may even be relieved because they knew the job wasn't right for them. Still, since many fired employees will be emotional and needy, you should try to be strong and help them to move on. The fired employee doesn't need to agree with what has happened, but they *do* need to accept it.

You will probably lose sleep the first time you prepare to terminate an employee. You may even get physically sick over it. If you're a caring person and know the employee really needs the job, then you probably will feel ill, especially if the employee has children who depend on the income from that job to put food on the table.

I have a very easy solution for all this. It costs a little money, but it's worth every penny. Hire a good HR consultant to walk you through the whole process. Consult your attorney on what laws protect you — and the person you plan to terminate. It may be hard to find the time to do this, when you're working 80-hour work weeks, meeting with customers, travelling all over the country and barely finding time to sleep. But make time for it — because, if you bungle a firing, it can become a major disruption for your business.

CHALLENGING TIMES

An important note when firing employees is that most states are "at will" employment states, meaning that either the employer or employee can break the relationship with no liability — provided there is no signed contract in place and the employer is not part of any collective bargaining group. When hiring is "at will," the employer can terminate employees for good cause, bad cause, or no cause at all. There can be time limits on this, in some states, so check with your HR consultant and attorney before you terminate anyone.

Even in "at will" states, you can't just fire people without a severance plan, a benefits plan and a plan to communicate the departure to other employees — and, maybe, even to customers. If you plan to hire employees early on, you can also develop this plan before leaving your 9 to 5 and therefore be fully prepared — at least in theory — to handle hiring and firing. There are many resources on-line to help you develop a plan. Write one up and then submit it for review by both a HR consultant and an attorney at your law firm.

As I've said in other parts of this book, DON'T HIRE FRIENDS AND FAMILY. Those who do are usually trying to make someone happy, but this one mistake could cost you your business. If it's hard to fire anyone, it's horrible to fire a family member or close friend, and when you do, the relationship may be over. So always take the extra time you need to mount a careful search and find the right person for the job.

> ☐ *Fire your first employee very carefully with input from both an HR consultant and from your attorney.*

RULE #21

THE 80% RULE

One of my greatest faults, as a beginning entrepreneur, was to expect all my employees to work just as hard as I did. That was unrealistic and naive. So take my advice: Expect great things from your employees, but don't expect them to be "you." Realize from the start that your employees have a life outside of work, which can impact their job performance.

I've always had a very strong work ethic, and I still believe that entrepreneurs, who start their business from scratch, without investors, should come with similar personality traits. An entrepreneurial environment vs. an angel investor start-up is very different. The people are different, the compensation levels are different, the loyalty is different and the level of employee commitment is very different.

This rule book is really meant for the person, not necessarily with an MBA, who has the great idea. The book is certainly *not* designed for someone who's been given millions to start their company, or to expand it. I need to clarify this because the 80% Rule just does not apply to the companies, with the big bucks, who can replace an underperforming employee with very little thought or notice.

This takes me to the 80% Rule and why it's so important to "scratch entrepreneurs." The scratch entrepreneur should use the 80% Rule in everyday life for all employees, both long term and short term. It really works. You just can't expect people to be giving 100% all the time – but

CHALLENGING TIMES

if you can *average 80%*, you will have a very successful organization.

In the life of an entrepreneurial employee, there will be a multitude of ups and downs. The 60% employee might be getting poor direction from a supervisor. In many cases, the employee's personal life is in shambles. There's almost always some reason that causes someone to drop to 60%.

Don't be too quick to judge — and please don't fire — the 60% employee. So, they aren't meeting your company's standards at all levels, all the time. But have they ever given 100% — or even 120% — at certain points in their career with you? I can assure you, as your business grows, if an "anchor" employee like this is in a slump and only giving 60%, you will hear about it. Their supervisors will have tried a few things and might come to a quick decision that the person is just not cutting it any longer and must be fired.

Hopefully, you catch this before it happens. Most likely, the 60% employee is making the supervisor's life miserable. The supervisor is working overtime due to the performance failure and just can't take it any longer. The supervisor is probably new to your company and doesn't know the history of your relationship with the employee.

Even though a supervisor may not be happy with the performance of an employee, it's up to you — not the supervisor — to make the final decision about any termination. No matter what, always think twice about firing people. Think even more carefully before firing "anchor" employees. These are the loyal, trustworthy employees who know you, and know the inner workings of your company. They've worked in multiple departments. You always know they'll have your back. They've helped the company grow and get you to where you are today.

If there was an employee who worked for me, I would always dig as deep as I could to find out what was causing their performance issues. Anchor employees don't have the same relationship with their supervisor because their

CHALLENGING TIMES

supervisor generally just cares about getting the job done. Anchor employees, no matter what might be happening to them, at home or work, try and protect them from termination and help the supervisor manage through the situation.

In business, you win — or lose — with people. So even as my company grew, I spent time at our weekly staff meetings discussing human resource issues. Yes, business strategy is important, too, but stay on top of hirings and firings, and pay very close attention to performance issues relating to your anchor employees.

On occasion, my executive staff would have to bring to me the news of an underperforming anchor employee. They would feel the pain the entire way to my office, knowing how I would respond. You will have the exact same feelings of loyalty to those key staff who were with you in those tough early years.

The executive might tell me: "Andrew is doing a terrible job and we really need to...."

"Stop!" I'd say before the last two words even left his mouth. "Remember the 80% Rule. We are *not* firing Andrew. Figure out what the problem is and report back to me."

It drove some of my staff crazy when I did this — but nine times out of ten, with support from our Human Resource Department, that anchor employee would be right back up to 80%, if not 100%. It took a lot of extra effort, but it was always worth it. And at the end of the process, the loyalty of that anchor employee was even deeper.

Another factor to consider, regarding performance issues and the 80% Rule, is that some employees won't grow professionally at the same pace as your company. The business may become more sophisticated, and may require different expertise in key positions. Some of the people who started with you will realize that their growth is limited and seek out other positions. With luck, those positions will be within your

CHALLENGING TIMES

company, but sometimes people just feel they need to change companies.

It can be as simple as wanting to shorten their daily commute, or maybe the person might want to work for a small company again. But sometimes the position has grown beyond the capacity of your employee. In these cases, do everything you can to find another rewarding position within your company where this employee can feel successful and operate at the 80% level — or higher. Doing that will also increase employee loyalty.

Finding a new position for this kind of employee pays off not only for them, but also for you and for the culture of your company. Other employees don't like hearing about anchor employees leaving. They *do* like to see you figuring a way to retain the loyal people who have been with you the longest.

But if any employee is consistently under 60%, right from their hire date, then it's probably time to huddle with your Human Resource Department, and prepare to show that employee the door.

☐ *Expect 100% and 60% from your employees, — but be very happy with an average of 80% overall job performance.*

RULE #22

CONDUCT BACKGROUND CHECKS ON EVERY EMPLOYEE

Always conduct criminal background checks on every new employee. It's a very easy process. You will need written consent from the new employee. Then get a copy of your new employee's license or passport before their first day of work. Hire a firm to do a criminal background check. You can also use one of the highly reputable websites that usually charge $50 or less. Once in a great while, you'll learn that your prospective employee is out of jail on bail, was accused of stealing in their last job — or worse.

I regret not doing criminal background checks in my first few years of business. We learned from a few situations the hard way. If someone isn't willing to give you a copy of their license or passport, that's generally a sign that something is wrong. It was most likely taken away. Even the most qualified and professional-looking people may have done something illegal. Find out before you hire them.

The problem with trying to do professional reference checks, submitted by applicants, is that their references will always say good things about them. A much better group to contact before you hire someone is some of their old employers. Many companies today will only let you speak with their HR Department and because of company policy and legal restrictions, you'll only get the applicant's start date, position and confirmed wages. It also may be a sign of a major issue with the applicant if the old employer

CHALLENGING TIMES

is not willing to say anything nice about the person and just stick to the rules.

The bare facts are not enough. At a minimum, you need to attempt to speak with past supervisors to be sure what the person wrote on their resume is true. Attempt to find out whatever you can about the person. If you can't talk to anyone to get details, then my advice is don't hire them. Something isn't right. You probably won't be able to call the current employer, as the prospect won't want to risk losing their job before you even make an offer.

As an entrepreneur, you may feel rushed to get the offer out and the new person on board as fast as possible, especially if your company is growing fast. But don't rush. Don't hire the first good person who walks in the door. See multiple people and, if there are several good candidates, keep them in your "Contacts" as potential future hires.

If the applicant is already known in your industry, call people you trust to get the inside scoop on the applicant.

And once an offer has been made and accepted, contact the new prospective hire's current employer to finalize the process and check references. You can always rescind an offer, if something doesn't match up.

Make sure to follow HR law when you do criminal and reference checks. Consult your attorney and get an HR specialist under contract.

☐ *Background checks ensure you're hiring the real thing.*

RULE #23

USE MONITORING SOFTWARE ON "YOUR COMPUTERS"

Most companies today use some form of computer monitoring software and control the Internet access of their employees at work. You and your HR people should tell the entire staff that company managers and executives can see everything that's done on one of "your computers."

Yes, that's right, you own the computers, so you have every right to control what is and what is not displayed on them. Monitoring software can help you gauge the productivity of an individual or the entire company. It can tell you how much time is being wasted on social networking sites — or employees buying Christmas gifts on-line during Cyber Monday.

But the most important thing is to find if people are stealing confidential information or, even worse, your hard-earned dollars.

Monitoring software even can provide historic information, if a laptop has been out on the road with an employee who travels. It's easy to purchase and load onto computers and it can help you head off the issue of wasted time before it becomes a serious problem.

Thus, controlling employee access to the Internet is critical today. You can do this with various types of software. It's as easy as coming up with a category list of accessible and non-accessible sites for your employees.

Installing this software affirms your company's values, including that of the focused pursuit of excellence. The

CHALLENGING TIMES

software eliminates distractions, increases hours worked on your business, and will make your business more efficient and profitable.

☐ *Use monitoring and internet access blocking software to keep your office productive.*

RULE #24

HOW TO HANDLE THE TOXIC EMPLOYEE

If other employees whom you respect are saying negative things about one of your employees, listen to those complaints and concerns. If they seem valid, prepare to take action. You may have a "toxic employee."

Toxic employees are employees who put their own needs and interests over all else, and try to manipulate those around them, by fair means or foul. Toxic employees ignore not only common decency, but also chains of command and company policy. They personalize disputes and judge others by whether they are "with me or against me."

Toxic employees harm your other employees and, ultimately, your company. They create, at best, a distracting side-show and, at worst, a traumatic dynamic with major long-term costs to morale and productivity. What makes toxic employees hard to fire is that they sometimes have a valuable technical skill, exceptional competence in some narrow area, or expertise of a kind that won't be easy to replace.

Unethical tactics used by toxic employees in the workplace include intimidation, the spreading of rumors, the silent treatment...It gets pretty brutal. When others in the office are unsure how top management feels about such abusive behavior, they will be wary of resisting toxic employees. Dealing with toxic employees thus requires leadership from the top.

CHALLENGING TIMES

You also need a strong company DNA, one which insists on professionalism, and the respectful treatment of colleagues, and which strongly discourages toxic behaviors, and weeds out those who indulge in them. These company values should be reflected in your training, in your management style, and in your company's performance evaluation system.

I was blessed with almost all hard-working, dedicated employees. But there were a few that you knew would have to be shuffled out the door. Performance failings are one thing, but a toxic employee is something entirely different.

Don't make a snap judgment that an employee of yours is toxic. Make sure you have multiple, credible sources before making up your mind. And, since toxic employees are often exceptionally litigious, be sure to talk with your HR consultant and your attorney before firing such employees.

But the bottom line is that you need to get rid of toxic employees — and you need to do so as quickly as possible.

☐ *Rid your company promptly of the toxic employee.*

RULE #25

HOW TO DEAL WITH DIFFICULT EMPLOYEES

Let's be clear about one thing. Difficult employees are not toxic employees. Difficult employees can be people who are inconsiderate around co-workers, weak in one area, but strong in another. They may be terrified by their employees, may come late to work every day, or spend hours a day surfing the Internet at work. Maybe they think some job tasks are beneath their "well-bred" background. This is just a sliver of what can cause an employee to be difficult.

When your company has reached full size, generally, your HR team can fix all of these cases, either through intervention or termination. Unfortunately, when your business is young, you'll have to fix them all yourself.

In the months or years before you can afford a full-time HR department, find an excellent HR consultant and keep them on standby. They will charge you a high hourly rate, but it will be worth every penny.

Don't over-react to difficult employee situations. Your employees are spending the majority of their day together, and there's always going to be some tension. Some "fixes" are worse than the problems they address. So be thoughtful and do your homework, or it could cost you greatly.

There is also a special group of difficult entrepreneurial employees, I call "the complainers." Complainers can be some of your most difficult to manage, but they can also be some of your most trusted and loyal. These personality

CHALLENGING TIMES

types love to complain, and often fill their day with complaining. Some are problem-solvers, and others just plain annoying. It's up to you to skillfully manage and motivate both kinds.

Listen to their complaints — they may have noticed something important in the office. But put the monkey right back on them. Get them to create special projects to fix a problem and reward them if they truly manage to fix it. Don't let them put a problem on your back and then walk away, unless you want to lose your business — and your mind.

Don't underestimate the ability of the complainer. They may annoy you with comments like, "I don't know why you are doing this," "That's stupid," "Our technology is terrible," or "I think the company has to do a better job hiring people." Negativity is a personal style, and some complainers have real talent.

Believe me, some complaints feel like a direct slap in the face. But don't take them personally. Some employees are very emotional. Learn the difference between emotion and disrespect. They may also believe that their long-standing relationship with you gives them the right to say almost anything they want to you.

Some complainers just need a little bit of support to fix a problem area. Most are very willing to receive the help they need. With most complainers, I had good success saying: "Well, what do you suggest we do about it?" Believe me, many complainers can identify and solve problems. Many thrive on that kind of job and can become invaluable members of your team.

☐ *Turn "the complainers" into problem-solvers.*

RULE #26

DON'T LET AN UNETHICAL EMPLOYEE IMPACT YOUR BUSINESS

Unfortunately, if you stay in business long enough, you'll experience unethical employees. While it may be very few in the lifetime of your business, you need to be prepared for them and to protect your company from them.

Most of these people will be with you for a very short time. They generally like to take confidential customer information and copy work product. Sometimes they will try and take some of your best employees with them to their new job as well.

How do you discover who's unethical? Sometimes an employee tells you about them. Sometimes monitoring software alerts you to the behavior. Or a friend in the industry might tell you that your employee is soliciting your customers or employees while planning to go to work for a competitor.

As I discuss in Rule 23, computer monitoring software will let you know before the person even resigns, what they are trying to take and where they plan to go, in turn, allowing you to show them the door.

And one final piece of advice: Have all your employees sign a strong non-compete agreement. Most such agreements last for the duration of a worker's employment and have a two year post-employment clause. They also prohibit employees from soliciting co-workers and clients. A

CHALLENGING TIMES

non-disclosure protects you from employees who try to give out work product.

We set this up in the early years, and it was a great success. While you can't control every situation, having a strong non-compete with every employee can really help with competition issues and ex-employees trying to steal your employees.

☐ *Unethical employees are a fact of life. Learn how to manage it and show them the door before damage is done.*

RULE #27

DON'T TAKE ABUSE FROM ANYONE ABOUT HOW YOU RUN YOUR BUSINESS

There are many types of people that you should bring into your business, but beware of those with big egos and a bad habit of telling you what you're doing wrong. As I've said before: Do a complete background check on prospective employees, conduct careful reference checks and, if you can, pay for personality testing before you hire someone.

If you do these three things right, you'll rarely have to hire a person with a big ego. And believe me, you'll find out a lot about the big egos from their previous employers.

You may also learn that what is written on their resumes is misleading or even completely untrue. Find information on their resume that you can easily check yourself and check it with former colleagues of theirs.

No matter what, if a possible hire comes through a family member or friend, be even more diligent in your research. Many times, people try and get in through the backdoor because they can't find a job any other way. You can't afford to hire people just to make a family member or friend happy.

While it's always good to take in everything employees are saying about your business, remember that your best employees will come to you with *solutions*, not problems. Any employee who constantly criticizes the way you

CHALLENGING TIMES

manage the business, has generally become toxic or has a very big ego. They're more trouble than they're worth.

At all costs, entrepreneurs should avoid people with big egos. These types of people think they can change you and mold you into what they want. They'll go to great lengths to try to control you. Bashing you is generally their last-ditch effort to bring you down.

While the big ego can very often find a job, due to their aggressive or slick demeanor, they just don't work well with entrepreneurs. You need people that look to you as a strong leader and are modest enough to realize that it's your business and you'll run it the way you want. If anyone consistently criticizes the way you run the business, show him or her the door.

When you look at a resume, if the person has been in the workforce for ten years or more and has changed jobs every two years, this strongly suggests they don't get along well with people. There could be extenuating circumstances, but beware. Do your homework before even considering that person. If you call them in for an interview, ask them carefully why they haven't stayed at any job for long. If you don't like their answer, don't hire them. You just can't afford the time or money to make a lot of hiring mistakes.

One final note: There may be serious extenuating circumstances that cause an employee to question your management. It might not be ego, but depression, illness or stress from a death or a divorce. If the person questioning your decisions inappropriately, has been a good employee for a long time, start by asking them, "Is everything alright?" I can assure you that those three simple words can make all the difference in how they feel about you and the company.

They will generally come right out and tell you about their problem because they want your help — and they need it. While it's difficult to delve into an employee's personal life, an entrepreneur's business is very much like a

CHALLENGING TIMES

big family. Your employees make many sacrifices for you, and, as a result, you should always try to be there when they need you. That's how you really build a culture and a business.

☐ *Find and nurture employees who look up to you as a mentor; and avoid those with big egos and a tendency to criticize.*

RULE #28

THINK TWICE ABOUT GIVING EQUITY TO EMPLOYEES

Growing rich through business ownership is the American dream. It's well known that during the 1990s, thousands of dot-com employees became millionaires overnight through their company's skyrocketing stock options. Less well known is that many of these employees lost it all when the bubble burst.

Just because the "hot business category of the month" is giving equity to its employees doesn't mean you need to.

Look at your industry to see if you have to give equity in order to be competitive. Giving equity is no panacea, and it can carry huge risks for the entrepreneur.

One year during the dot.com era, I considered implementing an equity program for top-performing employees. It seemed the thing everyone was doing to build business quickly. Years later, as I prepared to sell the business, I remember thinking: "Thank God, I didn't do it." Giving equity to employees can lock you in with people who can upset the culture and your future payout in a sale. If an employee with equity gets fired or quits, you open yourself up to financial and litigation problems. They can demand a buyout of their equity share, which may be tough in a down year. And if you give equity to one employee, others will expect the same.

I also explored giving phantom stock to my employees. Phantom stock, favored by close-knit or family-owned businesses, is a way to give employees a payment/bonus at the time of a sale without giving them real equity shares. After

CHALLENGING TIMES

a vesting period, the employee receives phantom stock for high performance. The employee must give up the phantom stock when leaving the company. Of course if the employee is terminated for cause or leaves on their own, prior to the sale of your business, they're not entitled to anything.

When I considered implementing a phantom stock plan for executives, my acquisition adviser asked me, "Why would you do that? Who really deserves it? You built the business from scratch. Were they with you from the first day the business opened? Have they stuck with you every bit of the way? Have they put their own money into the business?"

Of course, the answer to all these questions was "no." My advisor made me realize that my wife and I had borne all the upfront risk, and so equity for my employees hadn't been earned and wasn't deserved.

It's more motivating to employees, and less complicated, to give bonuses for individual performance. Make them discretionary and give them only to your best employees. When you give annual bonuses to all your employees, they come to expect it. Bad feelings can develop if you give everyone a great bonus one year, but no similar bonuses the following year. Employees can worry about the company's prospects or grumble at what seems to them tightfisted management. Give bonuses to those who really deserve it-for a job well done. Do it any time during the year and don't give bonuses out to multiple people at the same time. Tell the employee it's confidential between you, them and their supervisor. If they're hard workers who have really made a difference to the company, no matter at what level or how long they've been with you, give them a nice bonus. But no equity.

☐ *Reward employees with good salaries and bonuses, but not equity.*

RULE #29

DON'T LET ANY EMPLOYEE HELP SELL YOUR BUSINESS – SELL IT YOURSELF

You can count on it: Over the life of your business, some of your employees, thinking they are doing you a favor, will claim to represent your interests in conversations regarding the potential sale of your company.

Why on earth would they do this? Generally, because they feel this sort of grandstanding serves their own personal interests, goals and objectives. They hope to find out if you have any interest in selling the company. Or they want to feel they are a company "insider" privy to information which their colleagues never hear. Or perhaps they're looking for their big payday and figure they just might get it at your expense.

They may have been approached by one of your competitors for a job and have seen an opening to discuss the sale of your business. Or they may have been at an industry function and discussed it, without any approval from you, after a few cocktails. It generally is a way for them to feed their egos and pretend to be powerful.

Anyone who knows about how to acquire a company knows that you only discuss it with the owner. Potential buyers will call you directly — not ask your employees for your phone number. So beware: When an employee says: "I may have a buyer for your company," there is always an underlying reason and motivation behind this.

CHALLENGING TIMES

Tell them coolly: "That's really not an appropriate comment." Or, if you wish, tell them flatly: "The business is not for sale."

In the last chapter of this book, I discuss confidentiality and who should know about plans you may have for the potential sale of your business. Bottom line is: Your employees should not solicit, or even know about, potential buyers. It's none of their business. If you've kept your plans confidential, the subject will never even come up.

☐ ***The employee who wants to "help" sell your business is no help at all.***

RULE #30

LEARN THE ART OF INTERRUPTING

Time is valuable. Being comfortable interrupting your employees when it would save both of you valuable time is an important managerial skill. Interrupt employees at the conference table or in the hallway and don't be afraid to knock on closed doors. Some may think it's rude, but your employees will understand that you have a lot going on and need quick answers. It may be for an important customer call, a clarification on a graph or PowerPoint slide, or just because being a bit nosey when it comes to company business is part of your job. In almost every situation, your employees will actually appreciate your interest and input.

At meetings, don't be afraid to cut people off. If they are making no progress, you should give a solution and help everyone move on. Although these kinds of interruptions may bother your employees initially, they will soon learn to appreciate the time saved. Also, if it is necessary, you can interrupt and authorize dollars allocated for something that may solve a problem very quickly.

I would also regularly interrupt by what I call "Management By Walking Around." Some days I would roam our headquarters for hours talking to people in various departments about what they were working on. "Kelly, what project is that on your computer?" You find out intimate details about important projects by being nosey, keeping your fingers on the pulse of your company. Spending time walking around and interacting with employees is a

CHALLENGING TIMES

great way to discover outstanding work that could be the basis for a promotion or to catch problems to report to a department head. And of course, the biggest benefit of this management style is that you develop a closer rapport with your employees. Your interaction might only be a minute or two, but it's those hands-on moments that build a cohesive team and trust in you.

☐ ***Interrupt to solve problems quickly and "Manage By Walking Around" to keep your fingers on the pulse of your company.***

PART FIVE:

GROWING PAINS

RULE #31

FIND THE RIGHT CUSTOMERS

Where do you find the right customers? Are they within a few miles of your business or on the other side of the Atlantic? We were a successful national company that ultimately grew internationally. Would it surprise you that, in the early years, I never spent much money on advertising and rarely attended industry events looking for customers? Well, I didn't. That may not have been the right strategy, but I didn't have the time or money to do otherwise. Running my business and being with my young family took all the time and money I had.

I'm not a schmoozer, either, and even when I tried to attend, a customer meeting or important family event would often come up at the last minute, and I'd have to cancel or send one of my staff.

As our business grew, it became very interesting and a lot of fun to attend industry events, accepting awards or speaking on the occasional panel. But it's easy to overinvest time and money in attending industry events. It's not required and, for a young and vulnerable business, it may even be a dangerous distraction.

If you're a *great* speaker with a compelling story to tell then, by all means, seek out speaking engagements. They may well bring you some business, and the exposure may also help your company to be better positioned as an acquisition target. But if you're not a good public speaker, and most people are not, just forget about it. Dozens of skills are more relevant to business success than public speaking.

GROWING PAINS

Try to headquarter yourself in a low-cost, low overhead city — but then seek out big customers in the major cities and metro areas. My company was in Portland, Maine — but most of our customers were in the New York, Boston, and Chicago metro areas. Cultivate the biggest and best customers from around the country.

Cultivating customers is an art form, but one which you should pursue in volume. Even two or three big customers can make all the difference in becoming a profitable company. Sit down with your staff, brainstorm about every aspect of your customer base, create a long list of prospects — and then go after them.

If you develop a strong reputation, you may not have to do cold calls or spend a lot on advertising — your customers may come to you. As with a great restaurant, you'll get business from word of mouth.

But in some way, shape or form, you've got to find ways to let people know about your company. If you're not going to advertise widely; if you're not going to attend industry events; if you're not going to do much public speaking, then find other ways to let people know about the awards you've won, the big customers you have, and how accessible you are.

Be smart about how you do all this. Observe what works and what doesn't, and apply those lessons. Do targeted e-mails, have a great website, avoid high-cost mailings, and be very careful with your advertising and marketing budget. The time you spend testing what works and what doesn't will be well worth it.

One good link to your website could bring in a dozen prospects. Don't underestimate the power of targeted Google and Facebook advertising. It's cheap and can zone right in on your customer target. Facebook now has over 750 million subscribers. What better way to get your message out, and find customers?

As your company grows, your overhead and payroll will grow, and it may feel like a hungry beast. If you're

GROWING PAINS

a dedicated business owner determined to avoid debt, you'll feel the constant need to "feed the beast" with new customers.

But that's good; it's good to think that way. Never become complacent. Remember, even steady customers can disappear. They may just be looking for a change or might have been purchased by another company with preferred vendors. The economy could decimate your industry. Anything could happen. So, always be selling, and never sit back and rest.

Your entire company should be thinking about new business. Find creative ways to compensate your people when they influence a new customer or find a new service to diversify what you do. Get all your departments involved — Accounting, Information Systems, Human Resources, everyone. Some of your best sales and marketing ideas could come from people inside those departments. Encourage everyone to e-mail you new customer ideas and to leverage any connections they may have to bring in a new customer.

THE ENTREPRENEUR'S RULE BOOK

Write helpful articles about your industry and submit them to local and industry-wide publications. Join PR Newswire, which specializes in the distribution of press releases, to get out important news about your products and services. All of this helps but, in the end, it will all come down to the people you have.

Make sure your people will represent your best interest and serve as Brand Ambassadors for your business. Brand Ambassador employees are key to bringing in new customers. They need to project a professional image and convey your message effectively to important prospects.

All your employees, at every level, should have an intriguing "elevator pitch" about your company's mission and its products and services. Emphasize this "pitch" in orientation, regular training sessions and in one-on-one meetings.

Don't be surprised if you hear back that the President of a major company interacted with one of your employees/

GROWING PAINS

Brand Ambassadors and now that company wants to meet to discuss working together.

Bad interactions have consequences too, so train your staff carefully, and make them understand the importance of everything you're telling them. You can't prep your staff enough. When you send them out the door to do their job, make sure they know exactly what it means to be a professional in your company.

Image and reputation are very important. If you have a Brand Ambassador who's poorly dressed or has strange quirks, say something to them. Don't let employees meet with customers in casual attire. It projects the wrong image. It may be okay for your staff to wear cut-off jeans and flip-flops if you own a surf shop, but not if you're running a real estate agency. There's nothing worse than going to a meeting or buying something from someone who looks like they just came from a keg party.

First impressions are crucial. No matter what you do, make sure customers and prospects always have a great first impression. Make sure your employees smile and look put together. That can be the whole difference between winning a new customer or not. The last thing you want to hear back from a client or prospective client is: "We found it very strange that your employee always has holes in his jeans and wears the same clothes every time he comes to our headquarters."

It's not so much the money you spend on marketing and advertising as what you invest in preparation and training, making sure your people are always smart in the way they promote your company and always project a professional image and do great work. That's how you win new business — and that's how you keep it.

☐ ***Prepare every single one of your employees to be a great Brand Ambassador for your business.***

RULE #32

FIND CONSULTANTS WHO WILL HELP, NOT HURT YOU

Consultants can be very helpful — if they specialize in your industry, or in a specific area of business.

Why pay someone $500 an hour to give you a general overview of what you're doing wrong? You know what's wrong. So do your homework and make sure that any consultant you hire knows how to deal in specifics and how to focus on solutions.

Why is it important to use consultants who specialize? It may sound good when giant management consulting firms claim to "do everything," but they may send you some young MBA grad and charge you for every minute and every paper clip. Large consulting firms are often helpful to large corporations, but most know very little about running an entrepreneurial business. So go small, and select your consultant with care — but don't be afraid to hire one.

Let's address some common myths you may have heard about consultants.

Myth #1: They'll ruin the culture of your company.

True, you must be careful with any "outsiders" you bring in to help organize your business. Bad consultants can ruin a small business, disrupting the management and culture so badly that the company never recovers. There's nothing worse than an expensive bad consultant. But you can easily avoid this pitfall by hiring a consultant who specializes in your industry or a specific area important to your business.

Myth #2: Consultants are expensive. Only large companies can afford to hire a consultant.

Of course, consultants cost money — but in the areas of growth management, finance and logistics, consultants can help you to make money by streamlining systems and raising your profits. These consultants can really make a difference in the future of your business, allowing you to take on more while still controlling costs.

Opening new divisions and facilities, creating new procedures, installing complex software and setting up reporting methods can be a technical challenge, so you'll need to find an expert that knows how to get those things done. That investment is usually one well worth making.

Myth #3: Hiring consultants is bad for company morale.

This is another common concern about hiring a consultant, and it's true that one side effect of hiring a consultant is that when employees see you bring in a consultant, they tend to assume something's wrong with the company. In an extreme case, it can even bring the company to a standstill. Your people worry about layoffs and begin preparing excuses instead of focusing on the work to be done.

Combat this problem with good management. Be up front with your employees and tell them specific tasks the consultant is helping your company with, like a new division or streamlining systems. Explain to your people how the consultant can help improve the bottom line, and make all of their jobs more fulfilling.

But whatever you do, don't let a traditional "management consultant" tell you how to run your business. I don't care how many fancy surveys and questionnaires they have. It's *your* company, you developed it, and you know how you need it to work, and what the company culture should be.

☐ ***Only work with experts and stay away from "I do everything" consultants.***

RULE #33

KNOW WHEN TO SAY NO TO A PIECE OF BUSINESS

We rarely said no to a piece of business. Constantly evaluate your customer base and your bottom line. When your company's growing and you have plenty of customers, don't be afraid to take on more.

The naysayers will say: "How are we going to do this?" or "We just don't have enough people" or "Our technology can't handle this." But you know what the business can accomplish and what it can't, and 99% of the time it can take on more. How do you know you can't deliver unless you try?

Having "too many customers" is a good problem to have. If someone hands you a million dollars, do you say "No, that's not for me"? Only fools say no to a good piece of business. You might lose a few nights of sleep and have to pay some big bonuses to get through it but, in the end, it will all be worth it.

Your company DNA has to embrace growth. It all goes back to how hard you and your people are willing to work. If you've created a "get it done" culture, your business will grow by leaps and bounds. But if it's a "We'll see how it goes" culture, then forget it. You're setting yourself up for failure. Your people should want to grow the business just as much as you do — and you should motivate them to do that, both financially and by your leadership.

Having said all that, there will be a few cases, where you'll find the customer is not a good fit. I found out, in our industry, the smaller the customer, the more work was required. If you bill by the project, not by the hour, that can be very costly to your bottom line.

Another time you have to say no to a piece of business is when you learn from a financial D&B check on a company that they don't pay their bills on time — or at all. Or if the company that wants to hire you is one of many new players in a booming industry, beware: they may go bust. We always played it safe and worked with big firms that had been around, and paid their bills.

Don't get too caught up in the business fads of the day. During the dotcom boom, there was money flying everywhere. Many companies invested heavily in servicing these dotcoms. We played it safe with billings and stayed away from companies with no history. Boy, am I glad we did. Entire companies in our business sector declared bankruptcy after chasing dotcom customers who couldn't pay their bills.

Watch for signs that a customer is financially shaky. We took on one dotcom customer as a test. Their first bill, for $15,000, wasn't a big one by our standards. When they didn't pay that bill on time, that was enough for me to say: "See you later." I hated chasing for checks, and there's no reason to do it.

So check out potential customers and make sure they can pay on time. If you're unsure and still want to take them on, insist that they pay all your fees and expenses up-front. If they refuse, then walk away, and consider yourself lucky.

☐ ***Only take on customers who have a history of paying on time and in full.***

RULE #34

DON'T LET A FEW BAD YEARS KILL YOUR DREAM

I'm now happily retired in the Florida sun, financially secure, but let me tell you: when I was running my company, we had some good years — and we had some very bad years, too.

People ask me: "What's it like to run your own company?" Well, it's tumultuous — and especially in the first five years. There will be some years with no profit at all, and some years that are bigger than you expected. You may have timing issues with customers and vendors, and you may need a line of credit to get through it.

So the first question you have to ask yourself is: Are you and any family member, partner or investor you're depending on — ready for a rollercoaster ride?

If the answer is yes, then congratulations. You're going to have a lot of fun as well as frustration. And if you work hard and work smart, financial security may be there for you at the end of the line. I always ask people starting their own business, "What's the worst thing that could happen — you go back to work for someone else?" If it doesn't work out as you'd hoped, if the business fails, don't beat yourself up, but don't give up too soon, either. Put everything you've got into it and enjoy yourself. Remember, you've taken a chance that most people are afraid to take.

Also remember: whatever you do, don't allow yourself to have a loss or go into a lot of debt. Control spending and make sure you at least break even. Cover your personal expenses, prepare your family for some sacrifices, and think long-term. It took 10 years for my company to grow significantly. Just because you had a couple of bad years doesn't mean it's time to quit. Don't let a few bad years kill your dream.

When you or your employees think you need to buy some fancy equipment or add another employee to the payroll, ask yourself: "Is there a cheaper, more efficient way? Do we *really* need to hire that person?" Most of the time you don't. Let your employees tease you for being "cheap." The real word for it is "frugal" — and it's what keeps your company financially stable, and what will eventually help you to sell your company for a big profit.

Have faith in yourself and in your company. The awful year that looks like the end, most likely isn't. You just can't look at it that way. The economy may improve, your industry may boom, your main competitor may go out of business. You may even land a big new customer you had no idea was out there. If you're working really hard and dedicating your life to the business, things will work out.

You may burn out at times, but find ways to deal with that. Work out, take family vacations or just go for a walk at lunch. If I hadn't worked out at my local gym, I might have been done with the business years before it sold. You need to take care of yourself and clear your head on a regular basis. You and your company will be better for it, and much more profitable.

My employees sometimes rolled their eyes when I went away on vacation, but everyone needs a vacation. You need it to stay healthy and to keep your business healthy. Take time off whenever you can. It's not easy to find the time. I always did it around every holiday and school break. That was also a quiet time for our industry, so it worked. And I won't kid you, I was still working while sitting on a beach or on a cruise ship. But I came home refreshed, and ready to tackle the next big hurdle. If you can't afford to fly off to some island, then stay at home, read a book and spend time with your family. But do what you have to do to come back to work refreshed.

Work very closely with your financial managers and accountant to evaluate your numbers on a regular basis — especially when years are tight. While you'll know without being told what's currently working and what isn't in your business, financial experts can guide you to make better decisions about the future. Sometimes, they'll explain to you that what looks like a bad year is not as bad as you think it is. So get good financial managers and a good accountant — and listen to them.

You'll be surprised how much you'll learn about your business and yourself in a bad year. You can actually get better from the experience. Work to fine tune your company, and think more deeply about how to grow it. That happened to me. I had a bad year, made a bunch of changes to the operation, found new customers, built better systems — and the next year we boomed.

☐ *Be frugal, have faith — and learn from the tough times.*

PART SIX:

ACHIEVE WORK-LIFE BALANCE

RULE #35

LIFE MOVES IN CYCLES

People can be great entrepreneurs at any age, but it definitely helps to start your business before the age of 40. I hit 51 this year and I'm not really sure I could do it all again.

While I don't want to discourage anyone from starting a company, remember that building your company into a success is going to take many years. It certainly took years and years to build my business. It took 80-hour work weeks and 10 years of consistent revenue growth to be truly successful. Not every small business owner needs to make millions and retire, but you also don't want to be killing yourself working at the age of 60. So don't start a business without considering whether or not you're the right age.

You have to consider your family situation, too. Most of us have young children in our late 20s and 30s, children who will barely be aware of the ups and downs of a business. You're building a family and a business at the same time, and that can be very rewarding.

My wife and I have four wonderful children who learned a great deal, early in life, about business and having hard-working parents. Our kids listened in on kitchen table meetings and would ask what project we were working on, or where I was travelling next. They'd sometimes stop by the office and play at my desk or play a game on our company ping-pong table.

It's nice to show your kids and the rest of your family that you are a successful business owner. You gain a great deal of respect from them and also a lot of personal satisfaction.

ACHIEVE WORK-LIFE BALANCE

You'll be surprised that, even at a very young age, your kids "get it." They can see you're trying to build something great and provide security for their futures. They also know you're employing people in the community and helping them support their families.

But if you wait to start your business until you're in your late 40s or beyond, you may have kids heading off to college, weddings to pay for, sick relatives to care for. You might even be having health problems yourself. You'll be having more stress, and less free time, than do most people in their 30s.

You also can't have your kids come home and hear you say: "Guess what, son? You can't go to the college you want, because I'm starting a new company." That's not good for your son — or your business. To be truly successful, you need the support of your family in starting a new company.

You can't afford to alienate them, so get buy-in first. Most of them will say "Go for it." Some may say, "I don't want you to do this, and here's why." If so, listen and take their concerns seriously. But if you get support and enthusiasm in the family, go for it. Start young if you can, and have a goal to retire by 50.

Certainly, if your life is filled with free time and you can devote the proper amount of time and resources needed to start a business, then do it. There's nothing stopping you. Plenty of people have started companies late in life and had amazing success. But the earlier you start, the easier it should be for you and your family in the long run.

> ☐ *Make sure it's the right time of life to start your new company.*

RULE #36

CLEAR YOUR HEAD BEFORE TAKING ON A MONSTER

Stress is one of the great challenges of life. It can make or break the entrepreneur and his business. After you get through a stressful situation, incorporate what you've learned. Use stress constructively to become more protective of your business, more competitive and, ultimately, more profitable. Stress can also take a physical toll, can keep you up at night, make you physically sick and, in extreme cases, even disable you.

There are reasons why I talk about managing money and family throughout this book. The worst thing that can happen to an entrepreneur is to lose your business and your family, too. Money problems are a driving force behind divorce and, while you may not realize it, your family could be at risk if you bring serious financial problems home to share with everyone.

Some situations are best left at work. If you need the support of your spouse, don't take problems out on them. Get their advice and take it seriously. Work on the problem as a team, and don't stubbornly insist on something that could upset everyone around you. Your kids don't need to know about bad employees, bad customers, and layoffs.

Stressful moments in business come in all sizes, from losing a major customer, to having a crazy employee threaten you in your office, to suffering through your first government audit. Remember: A successful business owner may have thousands of employees and a similar number of customers. With all those people, it's just a matter of time before you have to deal with a very stressful situation.

Don't try and take on every big issue alone. Ask your executive group and your employees to help devise solutions. What you think is a big issue, may not be.

When you have a significant problem, get your staff to help figure it out, but don't be afraid to talk with experts outside your company. Most of all, learn from the problem, and adapt your policies or behavior, so it doesn't happen again.

In a crisis, whatever you do, don't react quickly in front of others with an "Oh, my God!" or "What are we going to do!" Stay calm and show your leadership with statements like "We'll figure it out" or "Let's meet in a little while and discuss this." Some employees love chaos and will try to draw an emotional reaction out of you. Don't give them the satisfaction.

The greatest single piece of advice I can give you in this book is: CLEAR YOUR HEAD BEFORE TAKING ON A

MONSTER. It's no easy task, but I believe it's what made me highly successful.

When you know you're about to encounter a giant obstacle, get out of the office or your place of business. Go to the gym, go for a run, go for a walk, go home and figure it out. Don't react quickly to anything, if you can avoid it.

I was a runner and a gym rat, and it saved me, and my business. I worked out at lunch 4-5 days a week. I'd start my day with a problem, figure it out on my run, sometimes with a wise friend of mine. I'd return with almost no stress and a clear, calm head to match.

I'd counsel a strange employee, terminate another, soothe an upset client, get briefed on a government audit, or stride into a meeting that could net or lose us hundreds of thousands of dollars. And I felt very grounded and confident in what I had to do. All because I'd worked out and given myself time to think.

ACHIEVE WORK-LIFE BALANCE

Some people say: "I don't have time to work out." That's crazy. There's always time. If you can't spare an hour, take a half-hour. If you can't spare a half-hour, take a quick walk around the block. It's not "a waste of time" and you're not "avoiding the issue." You're making a wise investment in clearing your head, and your company will be the better for it.

☐ ***Before any major business decision, de-stress by taking time for yourself.***

RULE #37

"SELLING YOUR BUSINESS" ON ACQUISITION-LEAVE IT IN GOOD SHAPE, BUT LEAVE IT

The first time I tried to sell my company, I did everything wrong. Said all the wrong things and did everything you shouldn't do when you meet with a potential buyer. Consequently, the sale didn't go through.

But I learned from my mistake. The second time I met with a buyer – five years later - I was prepared. The sale went through in a multimillion-dollar deal that left me never having to worry about money again. Selling a company right is very important. Here are things you need to do and some pitfalls to avoid, which can help you sell your company for millions.

Preparing to Sell

It starts with a careful plan. I had a 10-year plan. My goal was to build a company that grew steadily at about 5-10% a year. And I did that. You must build your business in size and scope and be well known in the industry for at least five years before you even consider selling it. No company worth its salt will buy your business unless it has a strong history of at least five years.

In the first two years of your business, find an acquisition adviser *in your industry*. Each industry has specialists who know how to find just the right buyer for your type of business. Talk to people in your own industry who sold their company and ask for the name of their dealmaker. Your legal costs will be much less working with people who understand how to get the deal done. Don't hire a local broker who buys and sells all kinds of companies.

I found my acquisition consultant through a business friend my wife and I had known in the marketing services industry. When I heard she had sold her company, we called to ask if she'd been happy with her dealmaker. Best phone call we ever made. The acquisition adviser she referred us to —five years before we sold the company — told us three things the company would have to show:

1. *Three years of strong financials.*
2. *A strong, diversified customer base. Seek out different market segments or industries that could use your product.*
3. *Efficiency of operations. Closely monitor your labor expense because this will be your biggest expense and can really impact the bottom line.*

We focused heavily on these three areas and, five years later, sold for a multimillion-dollar figure to Omnicom

Group, a worldwide leader in advertising and marketing services.

Start the selling process early, and plan for it. Your success depends on it. From the beginning, purchase accounting software, like QuickBooks, to track expenses, revenues, and especially profitability.

Work daily with your CFO/Accountant over the life of your business. It's easy to slough off supervision of profits, expenses, and cash flow to your CFO or accountant. Don't do this. If you want to sell your business, get in the habit of personally monitoring cash flow and profits, and controlling expenses daily.

To be considered for acquisition, you need strong profit margins. Why should a company buy a business that only shows 5-15% profit margins? They can make that much by re-investing in their own businesses — or they can buy one of your rivals. Set incremental goals to reach yearly profit margins and watch your budget like a hawk and keep your payroll lean.

Don't overpay yourself. A large CEO salary hurts the profits of your company. And the bottom line is crucial to the acquisition.

Master early on the meaning of the terms "EBITA" and "EBITDA." Understanding how a potential buyer views your company's earnings is crucial to the sale of your business. The EBITA and EBITDA figures in your financial statement are essential to your company's valuation by a buyer.

The acronym "EBITA" refers to a company's earnings before the deduction of interest, tax and amortization expenses. It is a useful indicator of efficiency and profitability. "EBITDA" is like "EBITA," but refers to earnings before depreciation as well.

Don't sell yourself short. Why sell the company for less than what it's worth? And don't sell for the wrong reasons — because you're tired of the 80-hour workweeks, or want to "find your calling in life." Most likely, you have already found your calling. If you're burned out from long workweeks, hire some help.

Find a large company as your buyer. A big company buyer tends to bring greater long-term security for your employees. Seeing their company get sold can be a stressful thing for loyal employees. A big buyer helps. It's much easier to "come aboard" an ocean liner than a dinghy.

I sold my business to an international conglomerate with over 1,000 companies to its name. The conglomerate had a philosophy much like mine — be fiscally responsible, treat your people well, and preserve its entrepreneurial spirit.

Keep your acquisition plans a secret. Don't tell any employees other than your CFO and outside counsel that you plan to sell. I saw companies in my industry make fatal mistakes in this area. One company told its employees it was on the market. The employees got all worked up, and had trouble focusing on their work. The company was needlessly damaged, and, in the end, the deal didn't even happen. In another instance employees learned through an employee at the acquiring company that their business was being sold. The last thing you want is for employees to walk up to you and ask, "Are you selling the business?" Tell everyone including the company that is buying you that you want it kept confidential. Most, if not all, professional organizations understand that.

After You Receive an Offer

The day my acquisition consultant called to tell me he had a buyer for my company was one of the greatest days of my life. My first instinct was to run out of my office to tell my closest friends. But I didn't.

The first time someone calls, wanting to purchase your business, don't get all excited. Above all, don't tell anyone. Your first instinct will be to run around, telling trusted employees and close friends. After all, it's a sign of your success. But don't do it. Even close friends talk. People just can't keep their mouths shut about things like this.

Talking about a potential sale can devastate your customer base. When customers learn you're selling, they might drop you as a service provider. You could find yourself in a quagmire of confidentiality, competitive and client contract issues arising from the sale. The buyer's accounting firm should consider these issues in the auditing process and implement a plan to deal with customer issues.

The potential buyer will also want the acquisition kept secret. They need to manage the process of communication to their executives, board, employees, customers, and the press. Selling to a publicly traded company requires an entirely different set of acquisition rules, which is yet another reason to have a great dealmaker.

I kept the deal quiet between my wife and I, my CFO, the acquiring company, the dealmaker, our public accounting firm, and a few lawyers right up until the announcement to our employees and the press. You shouldn't tell anyone until the deal is signed and the first payment has been wired.

We were honestly able to tell our employees that this was a good thing for the future of the business. The company doubled its profits in just a few short years during my earn-out period. That was wonderful for both my personal financial success and for the success and growth of my employees.

Obtain an earn-out acquisition. This means you stay with the company for a contracted period of time after the initial sale, and are paid based on the financial success of the company over that time period. Being acquired by a larger company can reap many benefits, such as new customers and reduced costs for employee benefits. An earn-out acquisition can create more profits and a bigger closing sale price. This arrangement usually allows you to run the business as you see fit, with payments based on the company's success or failure.

A one-time sale — "Here's the cash; you can go now" — is rarely done anymore. Most big companies will want you to run the company for an extended period of time. For those that don't, look very carefully at the price you're offered and be sure, for the sake of your employees, that the company will continue to prosper.

Create a great executive team who can run the business, as you would have. I built this team over a five-year period. Deciding who can lead the company and maintain the culture is no easy task. Look to those that have been with you the longest and helped most to build the business. They understand what makes the company thrive.

Leaving it in good shape means making sure the ownership is fully transitioned. Our transition took about three years. No one person has to run the company. There must be an ultimate decision maker, but make sure experts are running all departments. I had a team of six – a President, Chief Financial Officer, Chief Operations Officer, Chief

ACHIEVE WORK-LIFE BALANCE

Creative Officer, Executive VP Strategy, and Chief Marketing Officer. Everyone in these positions were my trusted allies. They believed in me, in the culture, and in the future success of the business. I was the CEO. I think it's up to the new company to elevate one of the team you have left to run the company in that position.

Stay with the acquiring company through your sale contract period, but not a day longer. One of the best decisions I ever made was to leave my business after the sale. I realized it would be best for me and for the future of the company. My goal was to build a successful business and go out on top. I did that.

So many entrepreneurs sell their business, but stick around after their contract is up, when it's not their baby any longer and they don't have the same drive. I always feel that's a mistake. If you can stay motivated and are profitable, then your job should be secure. My advice is — go out on top. Win top industry awards, and sell for a fair price. Find a great place to retire and leave it all behind.

And I mean leave it. Resist the urge to get updates about how the business is doing, or how it's being run. That's just gossip, which doesn't do you or your ex-employees any good. They need to move on, and so do you.

☐ *Start the selling process early, and plan for it. Find a dealmaker in your business sector, interview several of them, check references, and then hire the best.*